Write the **compound word**.

____

Which word begins with the same sound as **soap**?

sun   cap

Circle the things that are **alive**.

How **many more** baseballs do you need to have **10** baseballs?

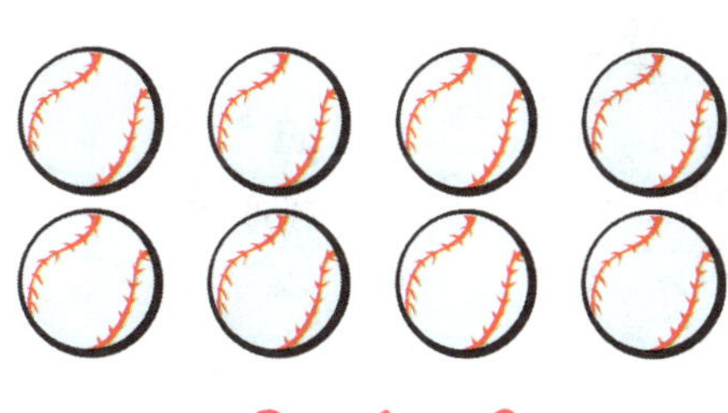

3   1   2

Circle the word that is the opposite of **over**.

after   under

before

7 sheep are in the pen. **5** sheep are in the yard. How **many more** sheep are in the pen?

______ sheep

Amy picked **2** more apples than **4**. How many did she pick?

6   5   2

How many **months** are in a **year**?

10   11   12

Circle the animal in the **middle**.

Write the missing **symbol**.

+   −

5 ___ 5 = 0

5 ___ 5 = 10

Finish the word **pattern**.

sad   happy   sad   happy   sad ______

What **3** things do plants need to grow?

water   clouds   soil   sun

Which clown is **taller**?

How many **nickels** are in a **dime**?

2 nickels   3 nickels

What do you use to measure **weight**?

clock   thermometer   scale

Which shape **does not belong**?

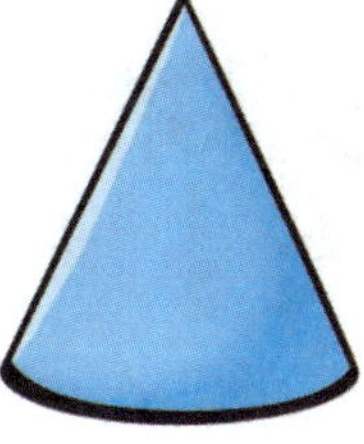

Circle the **verb** in the sentence.

Jake hit the ball.

Which object is a **cylinder**?

What measures **temperature**?

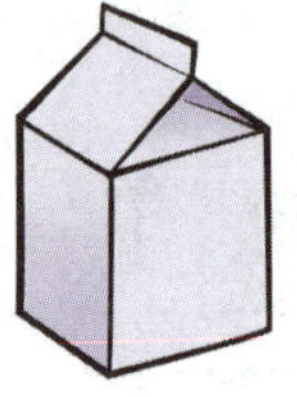

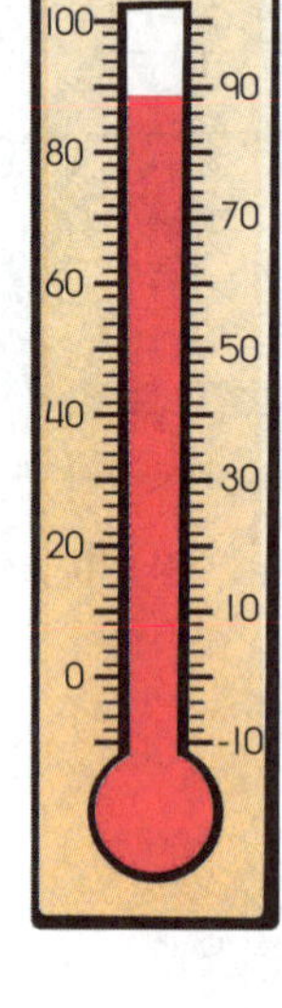
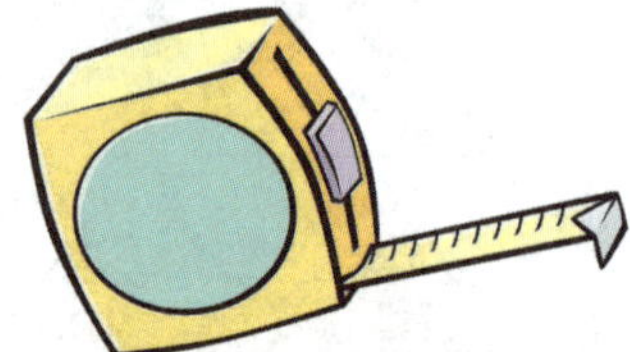

Circle the **5 vowels** in the alphabet.

a b c d
e f g h
i j k l m
n o p q
r s t u v
w x y z

Change the first letter in **hat** to make **2** new words.

____ at   ____ at

The cookie cost **20¢**. Can you buy it?

yes   no

8

Count by **5**'s. Fill in the missing numbers.

5 10 _____ 20 _____ 30 _____ 40

60 _____ 70 75 _____ 85 _____ 95

What does this sentence **mean**?

Don't bug me!

Don't _______ me.

bother   forget

The movie starts at **5:00 PM**. It is **2** hours long. At what time does the movie **end**?

_______ o'clock

How many **miles** is it from Ferry to Perry?

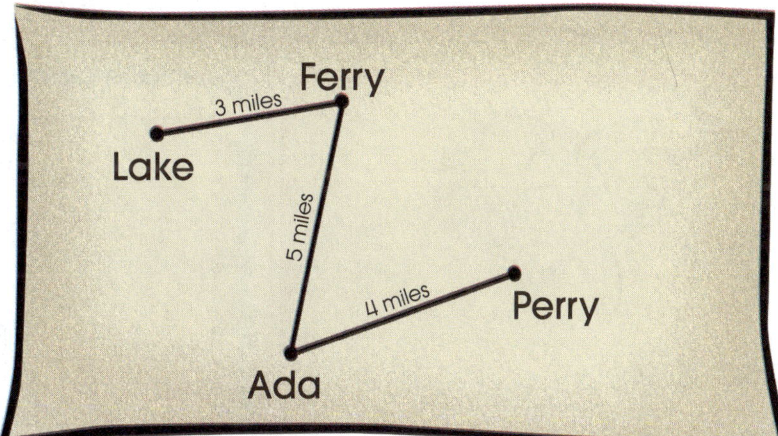

_____miles

   Little Thinkers First Grade

Underline the words that need a **capital letter**.

sara named her puppy pal.

Which **vowel sound** does the letter **Y** have in these pictures?

i   e

Where is the pot of gold?

4C   5G   2F

Whales are _____.

fish   mammals

Which is bigger?

a town   a city

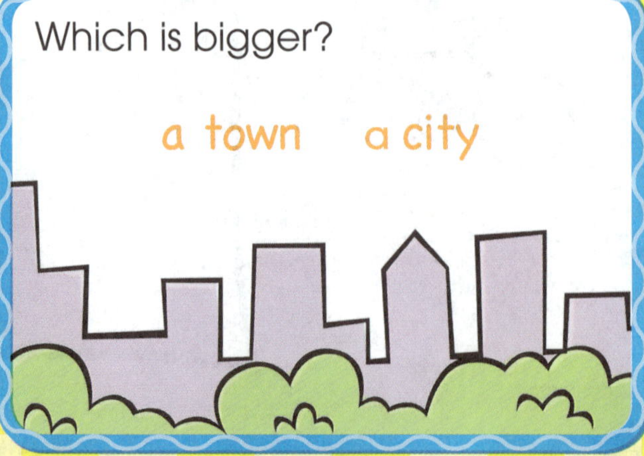

Which word is the **opposite** of **easy**?

The test was ______.

hard   simple

Cross out the word that **does not belong**.

foot   hand   home   leg

Which word means **more than 1 leaf**?

leafs   leaves

Circle the word that connects the two sentences.

I have a cat.
I have a dog.

I have a cat and a dog.

Circle two words that **rhyme**.

van   plane   train

Do these words have the **short** or **long e** sound?

seal   tree   key

long e   short e

Which word has the **same meaning** as **start**?

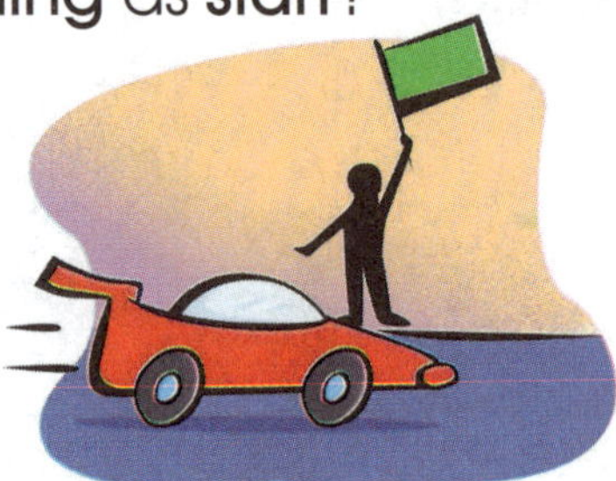

It is time to ____ the race.

end   begin

The Earth is a ____.

sphere   circle

Count by **2**'s. Fill in the missing numbers.

2 4 ____ ____ ____ ____ 14

24 ____ 28 30 ____ 34 ____ 38

Add the letter that makes bug mean **more than 1** bug.

bug ____

Add the letter that makes flower mean **more than 1** flower.

flower ____

How **many** hamburgers were eaten? Count the **tally** marks.

____

How **much time** would it take you to eat a hot dog?

5 hours   15 minutes

What number is in the **tens** place?

145 _______

224 _______

Circle the 4 pictures that have the "**or**" sound.

Which clock has the **minute hand** on 5?

Which word means **there is**?

_____ room for one more.

There's   Theirs

Do these pictures **rhyme**?

yes   no

Circle the shape that fits.

What do you use to measure **volume**?

calender

ruler

measuring cup

Which number has a five in the **ones** place?

27 52 59

14 63 25

Circle the **noun** in the sentence.

My sister is six.

Which word has the same **beginning sound** as thirty?

think   train

Draw and color the missing shape to complete the pattern.

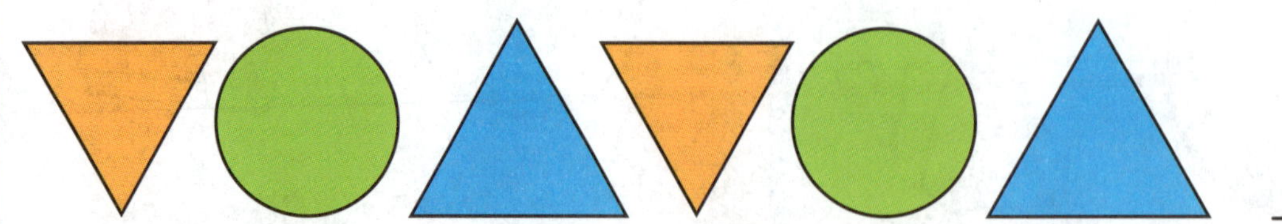

Circle the objects you can **roll**.

  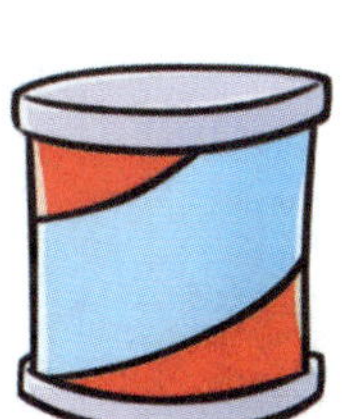 

Circle the 4 pictures that have the "**ir**" sound.

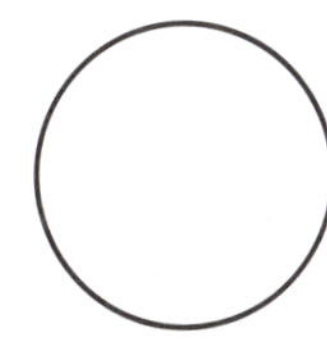 

Order the numbers from the **least** to the **greatest**.

54   18   63   31

___   ___   ___   ___

Which word **describes** snow?

Snow is ____.

cold   sharp

Is there enough money to **buy** the item?

yes

no

55¢   ___ ___ ___ ___ ___

Frogs begin life in _____.

water   trees

In which **season** do leaves fall from the trees?

winter   fall   summer

Circle the 4 pictures that have the "**ow**" sound.

Fill in the letters **ed** to make 3 action words **past tense**.

What number is **greater**?

61

forty-six

Which clock shows **12:30**?

Color **10** balls. How many **are left**?

___1___ ten   ______ ones   How many in all? ______

Is there **enough** money to buy the item?

yes   no

Birds are pretty.

fact   opinion

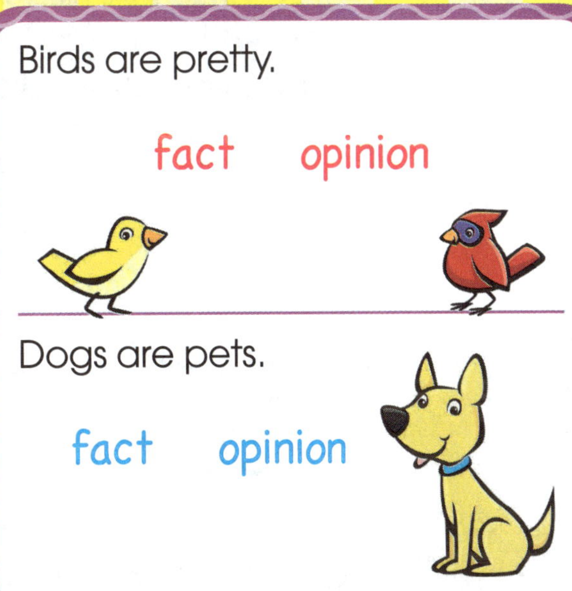

Dogs are pets.

fact   opinion

Sally bought **5** toy boats. Check the boxes she bought.

Which vowel sound do you hear in **tube**?

long u   short u

Which **sense** is being used?

touch   taste   hear

Which kind of pet does Pat like? ____________________

Which kind of pet does Carl like? ____________________

Which kind of pet does Jamar like? ____________________

dog   both   cat

Sam   Justin

Chad   Kate

Jamar

Pat   Carl

Janet

Kayla   Tamara

Can you see air?

yes   no

Do these pictures **rhyme**?

yes   no

Cross out the word that **does not belong**.

book

ruler

pencil

taco

Make words that begin with **ch**. Draw a line from the word to the picture word.

______ ______ick

______ ______erry

______ ______air

Which word begins with the **soft** "c" sound in **city**?

cent   candy

Circle the picture that shows $\frac{2}{3}$ of the pizza colored.

Circle **true** or **false**.

Insects can fly.

true   false

A plant is alive.

true   false

Write a word that finishes the sentences.

I ______ popcorn.

I do not ______ peas.

Which word means the **opposite** of **empty**?

full   wide

Which shape is a **cube**?

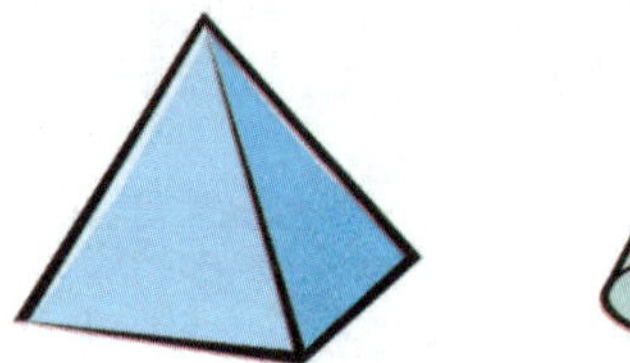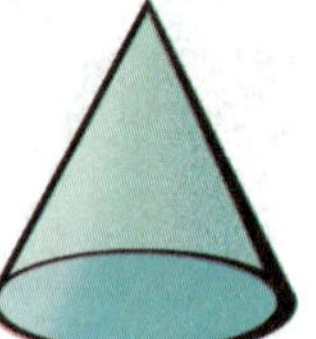

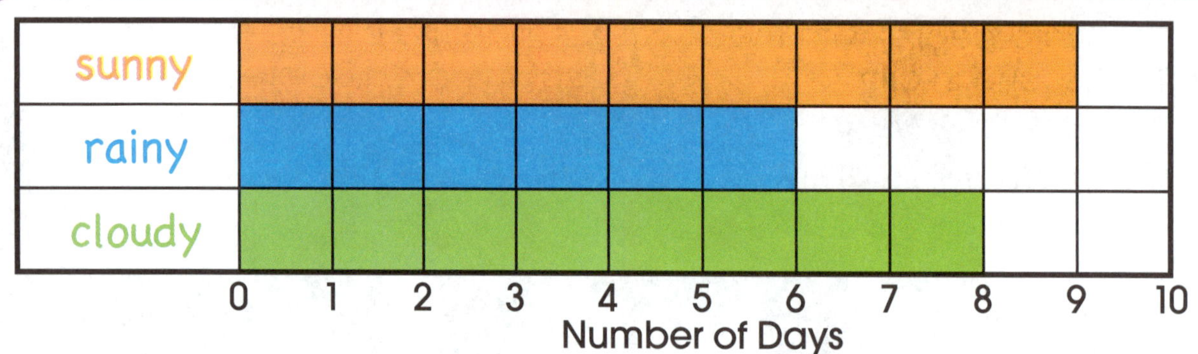

How many days are sunny ? ____

How many days are rainy ? ____

How many days are cloudy ? ____

Write the **difference**.

10	24	36
− 7	− 2	− 4

Shoes are to feet as mittens are to ______.

hands   boots

Which 2 pictures **rhyme**?

Number the pictures in **1, 2, 3** order to show what happens **first**, **next**, and **last**.

____

____

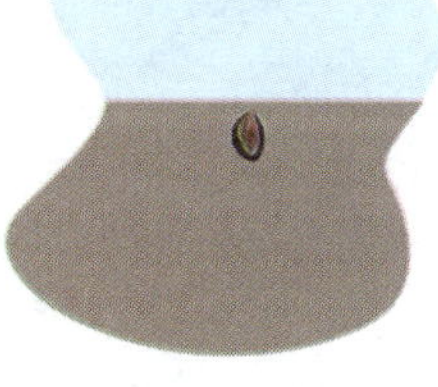

____

Which **plural** word for penny is correct?

pennies   pennys

Circle the correct **end mark**.

Can you come with me

. ? !

____

Ask your mother

. ? !

____

Hurry and ask her now

. ? !

Which **odd** number comes after **7**?

10   9   11

Circle **true** or **false**.

An hour is 60 minutes.

true   false

Count by **5's**. Fill in the missing numbers.

5 _____ 15 _____ 25 _____ 35 _____

Circle the **noun** in the sentence.

The dog ran away.

Which **sense** is being used?

touch   taste   hear

Which weighs **more than** a **pound**?

stamp   mouse   pumpkin

Write a shorter way to say the sentence.

I can not hear you.

I _______ hear you.

Which one hopped the **shortest** distance?

Is there enough money to **buy** the item?

yes

no

___ ___ ___ ___ ___

Which clock has the **hour hand** on **9**?

Circle the **verb** in the sentence.

The bird flew away.

Circle **true** or **false**.

Dinosaurs are extinct.

true   false

The winning number is between 40 and 50.
Circle the person with the winning card.

Circle **true** or **false**.

Insects begin life as eggs.

true   false

It's a home run! What sport is it?

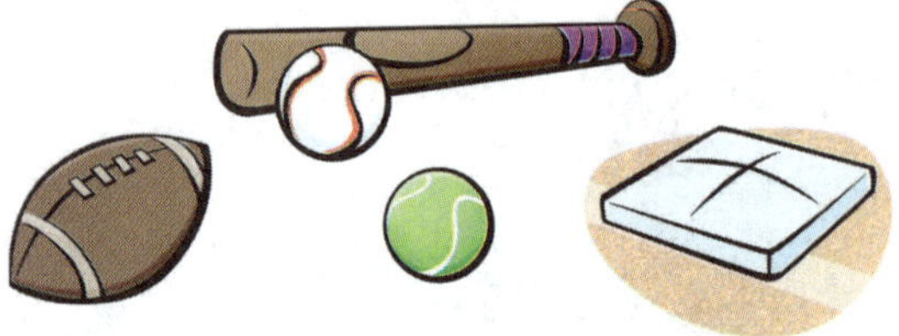

soccer   baseball

Circle who is in the **middle**.

Add **st** to make a word.
Draw a line from the word
to the picture word.

_____ ar

_____ op

_____ ing

_____ ool

_____ tens   _____ ones

How many s? _____

What words **rhyme** with **bug**?

sun   hug   rug

Count by **10's**. Fill in the missing numbers.

10 20 _____ 40 50 _____ 70 _____ 90

100 _____ 120 _____ 140 _____ 160

Which shape has **4 equal** sides? Trace.

square   rectangle

Which mark do you put at the end of a **telling** sentence?

It is a cloudy day

. ? !

Write the numbers. Write < or > in the circle to show which is **greater**.

_____   _____

How much does an orange cost? Count.

15¢   20¢   25¢

Circle the correct spelling.

Who _____ the game?

one   won

Fill in the last column of the graph. The first one is done for you.

Children	Number of Fish: = 2 fish	Number of Fish
Tom	🐟 🐟 🐟	6
Abby	🐟 🐟 🐟 🐟 🐟	
Tia	🐟	
Sam	🐟 🐟	
Alex	🐟 🐟 🐟 🐟	

How many days are in a week?

6   5   7

What word has the same sound as **new**?

bus   blue

Order the numbers from the **least** to the **greatest**.

12   10   15   13

___   ___   ___   ___

19   29   16   25

___   ___   ___   ___

Circle two words that **rhyme**.

whale   car   snail

Which word is the **opposite** of **open**?

Mr. Adams ______ the door.

closed   locked

8 cats are on your bed.
2 jump off.
How many are left on your bed?

______

Circle **true** or **false**.
The sun gives us heat and light.

true   false

Underline the **describing** word in the sentence.

I saw three goats.

Phone **begins** with which letter sound?

p f

Write the missing letter to make two words.

Which snake is the longest?

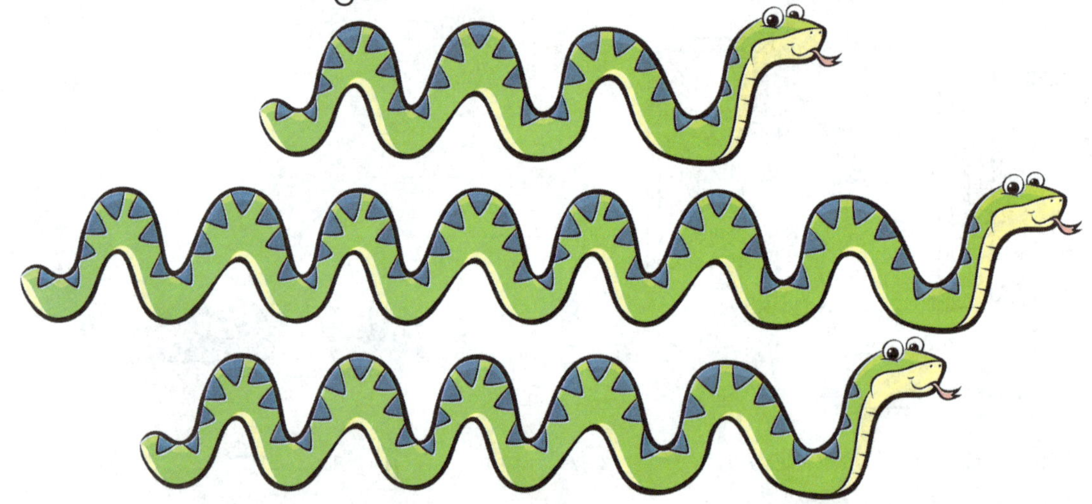

Which picture begins with **fl**?

Circle the matching time.

What can you **taste**?

What time of the year is it?

winter   summer

Write the number of corners.
Check the shape that has **more**.

________ corners

________ corners

Which word is the **opposite** of **front**?

back   before

Which word **describes** a kitten?

A kitten is very _____.

soft   hard

Which word has the same sound as **toy**?

ball   boy

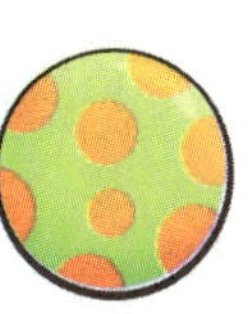 

Use the code to write words for the clues.

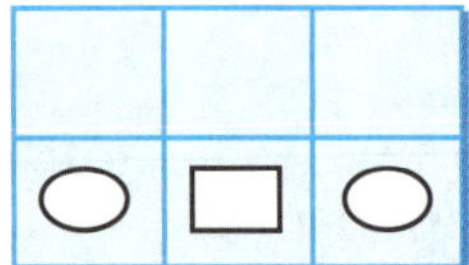

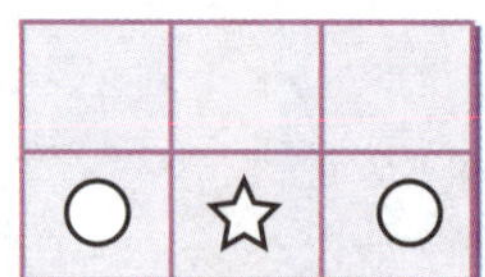

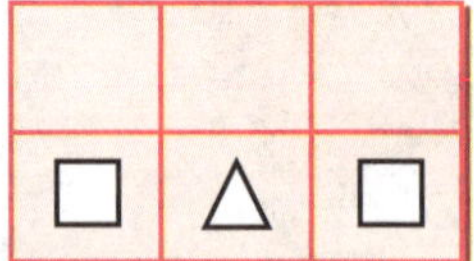

How much of the pizza was eaten?

$\dfrac{1}{4}$ $\dfrac{1}{2}$ $\dfrac{1}{3}$

Which shape is a **cone**?

Which word **does not belong**?

hop   jump   happy   run

Which weighs **more than a pound**?

Write the time.

______________   ______________   ______________

Which one **is not** a square?

Which picture **begins** with the soft "**g**" sound in **gym**?

Circle the **compound word** these two pictures make.

starfish   goldfish

Which number is **greater**?

54   64

____

68   86

Draw and color the missing picture to complete the **pattern**.

   _______  

Make a word that **rhymes** with **net**.

_____ et

Which word **describes** a mouse?

tiny   long

Mike has **10** marbles. Jack gave him **10** more.

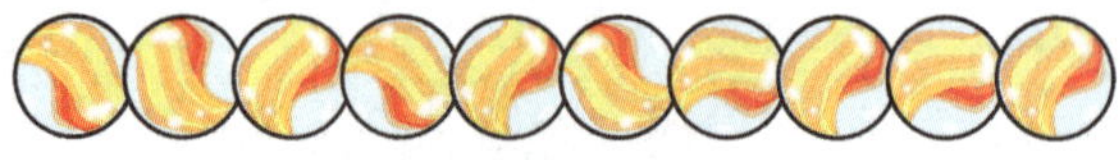

How many does he have **in all**?

20   25   30

Say the word. How many **syllables** do you hear?

monkey

1   2   3

Underline the words that need a **capital letter**.

susan and jan are friends.

elephant

1   2   3

Circle the **verb** in the sentence.

Jackson walked to school.